Profitable New Cake Decora

C000093329

Profitable New Cake Decorating Business

Lee Lister is a Business Consultant with more than 25 year's consultancy experience for many household names. She is known as The Bid Manager or The Biz Guru.

From an early age she began an unparalleled journey through business consulting that continues to span across the UK, USA, Europe and Asia. She has consulted for many companies all over the world. Specialising in business change management, start up consultancy and trouble shooting. She is highly skilled in seminars, lectures and corporate presentations on business, project management and bid management. Lee's experience in marketing and internet marketing is also keenly sought after.

She is a prolific published writer of books, ebooks and articles on business, entrepreneurship and bid management. She can easily be found on major search engines and Amazon.

Profitable New Cake Decorating Business

Learn how to set up a profitable business, understand how to overcome the strains and stresses of a new company and become a Successful Entrepreneur.

www.ProfitableNewBusiness.com

Author: Lee Lister

First published in Great Britain in 2009 as Start My New Cake Decorating Business –now greatly enhanced.

Published by: Biz Guru Ltd

Photo Copyright: © dethchimo

ISBN: 978-0-9563861-6-8

This book is dedicated to my daughter Kerry Lister for whom I have always strived to be my best.

Other books available include:

Entrepreneur's Apprentice

How Much Does It Cost To Start A Business?

Proposal Writing For Smaller Businesses

Profitable New Party Selling Business

Profitable New Cake Decorating Business

Profitable New Manicurist Business

Profitable New Quilting Business

Profitable New Bottled Water Business

Profitable New T Shirt Printing Business

Contents

Legal Notice

We do not believe in get rich quick schemes. We do believe that business is equal parts of inspiration, hard work and luck. We ensure that every book that we sell will be interesting and useful to our clients. Every effort has been made to accurately represent our product and it's potential and they are not intended to guarantee that anyone will achieve the same results.

Please remember that each individual's success depends on their background, dedication, desire, and motivation. As with any business endeavour, there is an inherent risk of loss of capital. **There is no guarantee that you will earn any money.** This book will provide you with a number of suggestions you can use to better guarantee your chances for success. **We do not and cannot guarantee any level of profits.**

This book is written with the warning that any and every business venture contains risks. We do not suggest that any one way is the right way or that our suggestions are the only way. On the contrary, we advise that before investing any money in a business venture you seek counselling and help from a qualified accountant and/or attorney.

You read and use this book on the strict understanding that you alone are responsible for the success or failure of your business decisions relating to any information presented by our company Biz Guru Ltd.

Introduction

For some cake decorating is a hobby, and for others, it is a career. The amateurs are those who find it fun and gratifying to bake the cakes and then decorate them for their family and friends, thus saving money by doing it themselves. With expert training along with good decorating tips and ideas, anyone can master this art. If you continue building your skills, you will experience the joy of making others happy with your expertise as well as building the basis for a good business.

When a cake is decorated in an artistic design it is pleasing to both the creator and the recipient. Creating a cake does not have to be a stressful experience, you just need to get creative. Don't be afraid to try new ideas and techniques.

This kind of business can be fun because you are dealing with people who are celebrating, but it can still be hard work and your MUST make sure that you have enough money to make a go of it.

Getting Your Business Started

Many people are thinking of starting a new business and cake decorating is certainly a popular choice. It is one of those businesses that you can start in a small way, providing you are able to obtain the necessary health certificates and business licensing.

It is also a business that you can run quite easily from home with just a telephone and a simple filing system and obviously a good kitchen and set of kitchen equipment.

If you have a good business plan, price your cakes to make a profit and are good at time management, this can be a lucrative business. Your main reason for wanting to start a cake decorating business should be that you are getting so many cake orders that you feel you can go into business and make a go of it.

Most countries and states require some kind of licensing and registration so you should check this out. You will also probably have to have a series of health checks and certificates. As you are dealing with food it is vital that you first undertake training in food handling and the appropriate health and safety rules. You will need to ensure that you have a kitchen that is both clean and well equipped to a professional standard and many countries insist that you hold health certificates and are regularly inspected.

It would also be advisable to have a background check if this is available. You should also obtain the appropriate insurance. It would also be good to have at least two checkable references. Once you have all of these you should take photocopies and put them together in your Sales Pack.

Your Sales Pack

Your Sales Pack is the major step in your business – it is what makes your business professional and moves you to the next level. It allows you to work with larger companies or clubs who want to buy your goods in bigger volumes.

The Sales Pack must contain a printout or photocopy of your terms and conditions, insurance and background check, references and your brochure.

In your terms and conditions you should explain the details of your working policy. This will give information such as: your hours of operation; when a deposit and full payment is due; if you will deliver or not etc.

All these details should be included in your terms and conditions in order to not only look organised and professional but also to avoid misunderstandings in the future.

When you first start you should aim at producing about 10 different types of cakes with various types of decoration and colouring. So for example you can offer:

- 3 different types of wedding cakes say with different shapes.
- 4 different children's party cakes such as "cartoon", "car", "teddy" and "pirate".
- 3 different celebration cakes such as "golden wedding", "engagement", "retirement" and "birthday".

Once you have made these cakes you should then photograph them and use these photos for your brochure and Sales Pack. You can then donate the cakes to raffles and good causes so spreading the word about your business.

Your Brochure

Your brochure can be quickly made up on a PC. Design a one page description of your business and the kind of work that you do. Some photographs of some of your cakes would be very helpful so spend some time getting good photos. Include your contact details and company name. Do not include too many words – just make it catchy, memorable and informative. You can include a couple of graphics which you can easily find on the internet.

If you wish you can also include a business card. These can be professionally produced from web sites such as vistaprint or from your local stationary store or printer. Now you have your Sales Pack

Uniform

It would be a good idea to give yourself some kind of uniform such are one of your T shirts or sweaters printed with your company name and one of your great designs.

Match your colours of your uniform and your equipment to your company colours. This makes you look like a professional company. Make sure that everything is cleaned regularly – including your equipment. You might even purchase a good box or bag to put your standard equipment in. If this is too heavy, then use a trolley.

Your Equipment

There are some supplies that are essential when you are thinking about cake decorating. The basics are several pastry bags, icing tips, a coupler to hold the tips in the bag, a heavy duty mixer, several sizes and shapes of cake pans, recipes for cakes and icing, mixing bowls, rubber spatulas, and metal icing spatulas, a sharp knife, and a baking tray. You will find a cake stand would be a big help, as it swivels so you can frost all sides of the cake, and bring the cake up and closer to you.

Later on you will want to spread your wings and expand your cake decorating and baking inventory. Below are some of the items you may want to purchase.

- Rolled fondant cake icing is a premium quality, non-stick, icing that is pliable and can be rolled out for cake decorating with a rolling pin or mechanical sheeter. This Fondant produces a satiny smooth and elegant finish to any cake. This product can also be used as a modelling paste to create decorative flat or 3-D pieces for your cake decoration.
- Buttercream Icing. Ready to use for cake decorating and icing.
- Hexagon Cake Pan. Also think about a Cut Corner Sheet Cake Pan, Petal Cake Baking Pans, Heart Cake Pans, Square cheesecake pan with removable bottom, Oval Cake Pan Set, baking ring, Round Cake Pan Sets, Wedding Cake Pan Set, Round, fluted cake pans and non-stick angel food cake pan.

- 3 tier Cake and Dessert Stand.
- French Chef Rolling Pin.

Other tools needed are:

- A professional icing smoother or thin metal spatula. This tool will help you to cover your decorated cake with an even layer of icing, and to make the frosting very smooth so that it can be decorated. This will make the cake look as if a pro did it.

- The use of decoration moulds is a very easy way to make figures and objects to use in cake decorating. You will probably want to start with the basic shapes like circles, squares, or triangles, until you are sure of how to perfect the process. You can move from that to flowers, numbers, and characters. Some moulds also have text so you can add a message.

- Icing bags are an absolute essential if you want to do any type of cake decorating. Once you get the hang of it, you will be able to use it as you would an ink pen, except it is held with both hands. One hand is used to apply steady pressure on the upper part of the bag, while the other guides the tip to make the decorations.

- The use of frosting flowers that are already made for you is a less time consuming way to add beauty to your cake decorating.

- Edible glitter and colourful sprinkles are a great way to spruce up your cake decorating design. These small additions could be just the thing to give your cake that finishing touch.

- Edible colour sprays are quite easy to use, especially when you are using a template. It can be the difference between a cake decoration that is blah, to one that has everyone complimenting you on your artistic ability.

- You can also print out edible photographs of the graduate, that fish that almost got away, or a wedding photo of the bride and groom, the way they looked when they were married to place on their 50th anniversary cake. The paper these edible images are printed on is also edible, so you can place the whole thing on the cake.

- A cake stand will make your creation stand out, especially a glass stand.

- If you wish to attend shows you should also set up a few "false" demo cakes. You can do this with boxes covered with royal icing.

You might also consider a message board in your office to hold both messages and design ideas you have found. Lastly you will need an accountancy package or MsExcel to keep your accounts and MsWord for your invoices/receipts and correspondence. Email will make your customer correspondence quicker and easier for both you and your customers.

A Few Cake Decorating Ideas

Did you know that the first cakes baked in America where small loaves of sweet bread? Look how far we have come. Home bakers should not be intimidated by the elaborate cakes being made today. You do not need to be a pastry chef to make beautiful cakes, you just need the know-how and practice. Of course the right tools will go a long way in your cake decorating endeavours. Here are a few ideas you might like to try.

Every cake worth merit starts with a smooth icing. The cake needs to cool completely before they are iced and decorated. To keep crumbs from ending up in your icing and ruining the look of your cake, start with a thin base coat of frosting that is not quite as stiff as the regular layer will be. Once this coat is on, set the cake in the refrigerator for 20 minutes. This will set the icing and any crumbs will be caught in this first layer. Now you can spread a regular layer of icing without worrying about crumbs.

Use an icing spatula to apply and smooth the second coat of icing. Once the icing is on the cake, start smoothing on the sides by running the spatula around the perimeter of the cake. One trick for smoothing the frosting is to dip the metal icing spatula in cold water, this will aid in smoothing the frosting. To smooth the top, dip the spatula in cold water and holding it horizontally over the top of the cake.

Start at the point farthest from you, holding the spatula in both hands, skim the top of the icing by bringing the spatula straight toward you.

Some cake decorators say learning to smooth the icing is the hardest part of cake decorating. Practice will make you a pro in not time. Once you have it down, show it off, even a cake without many decorations that is clean and smooth will make a perfectly elegant offering.

Instead of icing, cake tops can be dusted with powdered sugar. You can choose to use a stencil for a more decorated appearance, or just the powdered sugar for a clean look.

Edible decorations are a beautiful yet simple cake decorating technique. The use of sprinkles, candy, nuts, and coconut pressed into the icing before it sets, will make your cake stand out.

To apply a textured look for your cake decorating, use a small cardboard comb, available in baking supply stores.

Piping is achieved by using a pastry bag fitted with a metal tip that is held on by a coupler.

This is your most important tool for cake decorating. You can make lines, words, shells, flowers, and many other designs on the top or sides of the cake. Fill the bag with no more than 1 cup of icing at a time, twist the top of the bag and keep steady pressure when piping the design.

Use your other hand to guide the tip. It is wise to find out everything you can about piping before you begin.

Fondant a smooth white paste, is used in complicated cake decorating. Fondant is kneaded and rolled to cover cakes with a sleek smooth layer of icing. It is also used to make designs that are 3-D. It is less tasty than butter cream, but the cake will look sleek and elegant.

Standing Out From the Crowd

I f you want to have a cake decorating business that truly stands out, your cakes will have to truly stand out for you. To do this, you should have a good idea on what it takes to make a good cake and decorate it. You should also know how to use a fondant as well as make icing flowers. Now it is time to use what you know and put it to good use.

Decorated cakes, as sad as this seems, are a dime a dozen. Most people go to the grocery store bakery where a cake can be ordered in a matter of hours and generically decorated to suit most people.

You want to sell to someone is daring enough to have a cake that stands out, such as one that is shaped like the Eiffel Tower or Empire State Building. Once you know the concept of baking a good cake and how to use icing, frosting and fondant, you should be able to come up with a few designs of your own.

Incorporate some different shapes and allow your imagination to run wild. Remember, you are only making a cake, not operating on a brain. The worst thing that can happen is that the cake does not turn out well. Practice making some specialist cakes that are unique and attractive. The more you can allow your imagination to run your art, the more unique your business will be.

You are going to have to pull off something more than the standard fare. The cake is going to have to taste good and look good. Actually, it is more important that it looks good. Average designs are out - unique is in. You want your cakes to stand out above all others.

You are going to have to become a whiz at making wedding cakes and dealing with brides. This is a whole subject itself. Dealing with brides is always pleasant, but a stressed our bride can be a difficult client that needs gentle handling.

Once you practice a few innovative designs in cake decorating of which you are proud, spray them with lacquer so that they keep their shape. They can be your showpieces in your shop. People will want to see your products when they come into your shop and such exquisite, artistic cakes are not easy to make on an every day basis.

Another thing you need to do when incorporating art into your cake decorating is to think outside the box a little when it comes to baking pans and shapes. Do not limit yourself to the standard pans. Learn how to make a sculpture with your cakes to make the shapes truly unique, even if it involves using unconventional cake pans.

Cake decorating is an art form. In order to be successful at this business, you need to be willing to experiment with shapes as well as ingredients and not be afraid of turning out a flop once in a while. Of course, you will want to make sure that all cakes you offer to customers have been tried and true so that you do not have a flop for someone's wedding as that would be a disaster.

Use your imagination as well as your love for baking to allow your cake decorating business thrive. And above all, incorporate your artistic creativity into your cake decorating business.

Mastering Sugarcraft

In cake decorating circles, sugarcraft is probably the most misunderstood term. What exactly is sugarcraft? To clear things up a bit, sugarcraft is a type of cake decorating that is three- dimensional. Sugarcraft is decorating that stands out from all other forms of cake decorating.

Sugarcraft is to cake decorating what clay is to sculpting. It is the art of modelling 3-D figures on a cake. The type of icing used in sugarcraft, rolled fondant, is dough that can be used to cover the cake and making cake decorations. Sugarcraft is rolled into sheets and draped over cakes, or cut to make ribbons, bows, and flowers. Fondant is made in advance and stored in the refrigerator in an airtight container until needed.

When a rolled fondant is prepared for cake decorating, liquid food colouring should not be used; it can make the fondant runny and unusable. It is better to use colouring paste.

It takes a bit of time to learn sugarcraft decorating, and the process can be frustrating. There is no set formula for sugarcraft, you will need to use your artistic eye, and practice until you feel you have it right.

If you are serious about mastering sugarcraft, it is to your advantage to purchase a DVD or video that will show you the art step-by-step. An even better option would be to take a class in sugarcraft, as the teacher can give you tips and feedback as you learn.

When you look for sugarcraft supplies, Surbiton Sugarcraft is an online store with everything you will need. Based in the UK, this company has so many items this article does not afford the space to list them all.

A sampling of their sugarcraft art and tools:

- Stainless Steel Cutters to Make: Blossoms, flowers, Leaves, Calyx, Micro and Midi cutters.
- A large array of tools that are food grade plastic and stainless steel such as: Ribbon cut from flower paste, ribbon insertion, garrett frill cutters, and plaque cutters.
- Sugar paste: This allows for a smooth finish every time it is used and covers cakes without cracking and forming craze lines. This paste is less gritty and oily than other sugar pastes and easy to handle. It is bright white and unflavoured.
- Edible Lustre Air Brush Colours: A Lustre air brush spray for food in a can. Works wonderfully for colouring sugar paste, modelling paste, marzipan, buttercream etc. Available in 6 colours.

• Sugarcraft rosebuds and roses: The rosebuds come in lemon, peach, violet, pink, red, ivory, white, cerise, and claret. They are sold in various quantities and are incredibly beautiful.

• Piped roses - These wonderful roses are a bit smaller and a bit different. They are great for cupcake decoration. Available in dark pink, pink, or white.

• There are many more sugarcraft decorations including orchids, cake pans, cake dummies, cake boxes, leaves, and flower sprays all made with sugarcraft.

Wedding Cakes

L ike it or not, if you are going to have a business in cake decorating, you are going to have to deal with some anxious brides. People should get combat pay for dealing with some brides as they are usually nervous as they worry about every little thing, longing for the big day to be perfect.

Wedding cakes are big business, however. During the time the bride is ordering the cake, she wants to make sure that everything spells romance and elegance for the big day.

The days of the seven tier wedding cake as seen in the movie "The Godfather" are long gone. Today, most people are looking for something a bit more subdued and elegant. Wedding cakes are still in tiers, but most of the modern cakes that are being offered by the decorating artists no longer employ those little plastic columns to hold up the tiers.

Instead, a series of pans are usually used for the wedding cake. The pans range in size and form somewhat of a pyramid. This can be square or round. Each layer is covered with fondant or icing and trimmed with pearls or flowers. This makes for a very elegant looking cake.

Choosing a wedding cake is quite a task. Tradition calls for a white cake with white frosting for weddings. In this day and age, couples are choosing their favourite flavour. This has bakeries and cake decorators striving to offer a larger selection of cakes. Chocolate, fruit, yellow, pound, and marble are some of the cakes made for modern weddings.

Some wedding cakes offer a different flavour for each layer. White icing, while still ordered, has made way for a wider selection of frostings or icings. Chocolate, mocha, lemon, and any other flavour you can imagine are used for wedding cake decorating. It is possible to customise your cake using all of your favourite flavours. How the wedding cake is decorated is a personal choice. You can have just about anything you can dream up put on a wedding cake including, fruit and even real edible flowers.

It is desirable, when decorating a cake, to make sure that everything on the cake is edible. Making pearls and flowers out of icing is not difficult and is something that you should have learned in cake decorating school. Having everything on the cake edible only adds to the allure of the wedding cake.

The one rule of thumb when dealing with brides and wedding cakes is that the bride is always right. She is allowed to change her mind 30 times because she is the bride, so be patient.

Wedding cakes are big business and can net you more of a profit than any other type of cake. You want to get the wedding cake trade if you are in the cake decorating business.

To get more wedding cake trade, take some samples as well as some fake cake displays to wedding shows. Wedding shows operate weekly throughout most areas and are a way for brides and grooms to find out the best places to get shoes, wedding gowns, honeymoon destinations and wedding cakes. Make sure that your cakes really stand out and that you set up a nice stand. The cost to attend these wedding shows is usually around $100 for a weekend, but the exposure is well worth it.

A marketing trick you can use is to give samples of cake to those who visit your booth. You can also ask them to sign up for the grand prize - a free wedding cake! Once you have their name and number, you can use a bit of telemarketing to try to get them to come in and sample the different cakes you make.

A cake decorating business is no different than any other business. In addition to being a decorating artist and expert baker, you also need to know how to market your business to get the most exposure and revenue. And remember that brides are always good for business. They may be difficult to deal with, but they are necessary when it comes to finding success in the cake decorating business.

Children's Birthday Cakes

Another lucrative business in the cake decorating industry is children's birthday party cakes. Children's cakes, including birthday and other party cakes, such as graduation cakes, are another necessary item you will need to provide, and provide well, when embarking on a cake decorating business.

While many people rush off to the grocery store to get the cakes for their kid's party, it only takes one person in the local clique to come up with something different and the rest of the parents will follow suit. While kids rarely care about cake or anything else but presents during their parties, adults are in constant competition on who can throw the best party for their little darling. This ranges from entertainment for the children to party favours to cakes.

If you a have never lived in the suburbs, congratulations. If you have, with children, you know the score. The competition is fierce. If little Johnny has a party where he gets a cake that isn't quite the norm that the local grocery store provides, people will be sure to want to know where the cake came from. Because when it comes time for little Janie's party, you can bet that her mother will want the same thing only better!

This is the way it works for kids' parties. No longer are children lined up to play "pin the tail on the donkey." Instead, the more elaborate the party and entertainment, the better it is....for the neighbours to envy.

You can take advantage of this trend by offering unique cakes for children's birthday parties and graduations. Use your imagination and come up with something truly unique. Do not be hampered by the size of the pans, either. Cakes can be cut, when cold, and made into different forms. And when covered with icing or fondant, there is no telling what you can do.

When offering children's birthday party cakes, the best way to get started is to offer to make a birthday cake, for free, for a neighbour's child. Make sure that your neighbour or friend is inviting a lot of other kids to the party as well as their parents. The children should be young. Older children rarely care about cakes or the size and shape. Little children tend to care about toys and games. Mothers of children who come to the party tend to care about decorations, how much you spent on the party, your form of entertainment and what is in your medicine cabinet. These are the people you want to impress as they will be the ones ordering cakes.

You may have to give away quite a few cakes to start your business, but it will be worth it.   All the advertising in the world does not beat a bunch of gossipy moms trying to out do each other when it comes to their kids' birthday parties. There is a lucrative business in cake decorating if you have talent, can bake a tasty and unique looking cake.

Children's Cake Decorating Ideas

Candy Land Cake: Make a standard sheet cake in your child's favourite flavour, in a rectangular pan. When it is cool, frost it with buttercream frosting in your child's favourite colour. If you can get your hands on a Candy Land game board, you will be able to fashion the cake decorating to resemble the board. You can also go to Candyland.com to see a game board.

The Candy Land game features peppermints, iced gingerbread men, coloured gumdrops, liquorice sticks, chocolate candies, and circus peanuts. If you can't find some of these items, you can use construction paper to make them, staple or tape them to an ice cream stick to stand it up in the cake.

Race car cake: Bake two cakes, one in a loaf cake pan and one in a rectangular pan. Allow the cakes to cool thoroughly. Remove them from the pans, cut the loaf cake in an arch, like the shape of the top of the car. Frost the sheet cake and place the cut loaf cake in the middle, centred to give the cake balance.

Ice the car with a different colour icing than you did the cake, red or blue are good racing colours. You should be able to find decorations in the store for this cake. Use your imagination; many times craft stores have some nice decorations. You can either use icing to outline the doors and windows, or string liquorice works well for this. Small chocolate doughnuts make good tyres for your race car.

The Doll Cake: This cake is very popular with young girls who still love to play with dolls. Bake a cake in a metal, oven safe, bowl. When the cake has cooled, turn the cake out, centred, onto a prepared cake board. The widest part of the cake should be on the board.

Use a butter knife to hollow out a spot in the top of the cake for the doll's legs. Once the doll is inserted, the cake becomes a dress for the doll. Make sure the doll is clean and undressed. Wrap the legs in plastic wrap before placing the doll into the cake, up to her waist. Ice the cake and the top of the doll to make it appear that the doll is fully dressed. You can purchase accents at the supermarket to jazz up the dress.

Profitable New Cake Decorating Business

You can use the doll cake and have a Barbie theme party, the race car cake to have a Car's theme party, and of course, you can decorate for the Candy Land party with huge gumdrops and gingerbread men made of construction paper to hang or affix to the walls.

Cake Decorating Themes

Everyone seems to enjoy cakes that are themed to a special occasions. It makes the cake decoration stand out, and look more professional than a shop bought cake. Here are a few ideas to try:

Cake Decorating Themes

• **Fun and activity:** These cakes are full of colour and whimsical design. The use of different shapes, Balloons, circles, stars, clouds, and other interesting designs will help to make your cake decorating the talk of the party. With the use of animal crackers, you could make a zoo or farm cake. Your imagination can take you anywhere.

• **A Little Romance:** Romantic cake decorating is perfect for sweetheart's day, Valentines Day, a birthday for a husband or wife, or a wedding anniversary. You can make any colour frosting, including the favourite of the person or people you are baking the cake for. You can add hearts, cupids, or anything that will remind the guests what the celebration is about. Use your imagination and make it a little jazzy without going overboard. Just a bit of glitter or candies that sparkle should do the trick.

• **Say it With Flowers:** The use of floral patterns in soft shades, are perfect for cake decorating. The addition of a few green leaves make this type of cake decoration an excellent choice for any special occasion. Flowers are great on wedding cakes, birthday cakes, mother's day cakes, and for other happy celebrations.

• **Cartoon:** Younger children (and some that are over 90) love cartoon characters as much as they love cake. This is why it is a great idea to combine both when decorating a cake for the birthday of someone who loves these whimsical critters. You can either draw them in icing and colour them in, or use moulds and fondant to make the characters. After they are made, they can be coloured before they are placed on the cake. So invite Bugs Bunny, Tweety, Taz, Mickey Mouse, Goofy, Garfield, Donald Duck, or any of the many cartoon characters that have stolen our hearts and funny bones, and are doing the same to our children, to the party.

• **Characters:** There are hundreds of famous characters to use for cake decorating. You can make any cake special by drawing in Dora the Explorer, or Blues Clues. Or you may want to cut up the cake to make the entire cake into a favourite character.

• **Themes:** Maybe you would like to go with a 50's theme, underwater adventure, sport theme, or a roaring 20's theme for your cake decorating. Use your creativity and find a theme that will thrill the person you are making the cake for, and the guests. You may want to have a masquerade party in that theme. Whatever you decide, have fun.

• **Motor Cakes**: Boys are usually crazy about trucks, cars, fire engines, boats, tractors, helicopters, or airplanes. Again you can use your cake decorating expertise to make a farm with a 3-D tractor, a racing strip, or a scene showing a fire being put out by firemen. Of course it all depends on what the particular birthday boy is fond of.

• **Animals:** You can also use an animal theme by cutting the cake to look like any animal, or draw in a scene using animals. It could be a zoo scene with several animals or choose one animal and decorate the cake with other decorations showing where it came from. Use your imagination.

• **Food:** Maybe you are making a cake for the opening of an Italian restaurant. You could create a scene depicting the building, or if it is for a chef opening the restaurant, a scene of the kitchen with different Italian dishes would be fun. You can also cut the cake to look like a hamburger, hot dog, taco etc... The sky is the limit when it comes to cake decorating using a food theme.

• **Holiday Themes:** I remember when bunny cakes became popular at Easter, Wilton has pans and decorating supplies for all holiday cake decorating designs. A heart on Valentine's Day or a 4 leaf clover on St. Patrick's Day is a wonderful way to say happy holidays.

• **Your Own Creation:** If you have been involved in cake decorating for quite some time, or if you are a novice with an artistic flair, you can create your own cake based on the theme or the celebration.

Whatever cake you make will be the centre of attention as cakes usually are at a celebration. It has become tradition to have an outstanding cake at every celebration. Knowing that you are the one who is artistic enough to make this cake, and the praise you will receive from others, will give you great satisfaction.

Cake Decorating Ideas

H ere are a few ideas for cake decorating that are so easy to achieve.

• **Flowers:** Real flowers have become quite popular in cake decorating circles. You should choose smaller flowers that are edible, and make sure they have been cleaned. It is best to use flowers from your own garden, or a garden that you know the owner does not use poisons. Rinse them in a lukewarm water bath and blot them dry with a paper towel. Make sure you pick the flowers right before you are ready to use them on the cake so they are fresh. If you would like to add a dewy look to your cake flowers, brushing on a bit of lustre dust will make them look as if they are wet.

• **Fruit:** Orange slices, grapes, mandarin oranges, etc... You can make these fruits look frosted by beating an egg white, and brushing it on each piece of fruit, then dipping it in clear or coloured sanding sugar. This has become very popular.

• **Decorations Made of Fondant:** You are able to use fondant icing to make beautiful cake decorations. You can choose to make flat decorations, or make them 3-D. You will find that you can copy designs from just about anywhere, and model the decorations as if you were making them out of modelling clay.

• **Ready to Use Frosting or Icing :** Frosting in a tube, is the new rage in cake decorating. A variety of tips can be bought to make different decorations. These tubes of icing come in quite a few colours, and can be kept on the pantry shelf between each use. You simply remove the icing tip and recap the tube.

• **Colour in a Can:** You do not need to add colour to your icing when frosting a cake. There are wonderful food colours in a can that can be sprayed on any light coloured frosting for a dynamic effect. You can tint the lake and sky blue, the trees and grass green, or spray the entire top of the cake to change the colour.

All of the above ideas are very easy to use. Anyone can achieve a great looking decorated cake by using one or all of these ideas.

Cake Decorating Tips

If you want to become a master at cake decorating, you will need training and practice. Even a person who is new to cake decorating wants your cake to look beautiful. My mother just made a cake and frosted it, she may have added sprinkles, and she wrote a happy birthday message with icing. Those were our cakes, they may not have been well decorated, but they were tasty.

Although cake decorating can be frustrating at times, it can also be very rewarding when you realize the beautiful cake on that stand is something that you created. With a bit of patience and a can do attitude, you will become and accomplished cake decorator. Here are a few tips to help you.

Some Basic Cake Decorating Ideas

Let's begin with the basics. The cake decorating tips that are essential and things that you need to know before you. You will need a workplace that will afford enough room to be able to decorate your cake without being cramped. You also need to be away from disturbances and you will not need to move away from because you will be in the way of others. The first thing to know about cake decorating, is the fact that the cake must be completely cooled before you make any attempt to decorate. If the cake is still warm, you will run into many problems.

The next item is to make sure you have gathered all of the tools and ingredients for decorating your cake. Some items you will need are: a syringe or piping bag, the type and size tips you will be using, and the coupler to attach the tips to the piping bag. You will need to plan how you will decorate the cake ahead of time, so you can have all of the tools you need on hand when you begin decorating.

To begin with you need to ice, or frost the cake with royal icing, butter cream icing, or fondant icing. To start with, make sure you place a thin layer of frosting over the top to hold the crumbs together. When that is done, you will frost over that layer. It is important to make sure the icing you use is the right consistency. If the icing is too thin or too thick it will affect the end result of your cake decorating. If you are creating a decorated cake and you think your frosting is too thin, you can add a bit more confectioner's sugar. Make sure you add this a little at a time as it can become too stiff if you add too much. If you feel your icing is too stiff, carefully add a bit more liquid.

Icing is used in different consistencies for different cake decorating techniques. When you are making roses, or any flower with upright petals, and will be piping figures on the cake, you will want to use a stiff icing or your petals may droop. To make stars, flowers with flat petals, and shell borders, you will want to use a medium consistency.

A thin icing is used for writing on the cake, and thinner, more delicate work such as vines and leaves. If you add about 2 teaspoons of light corn syrup to your icing, you will find the icing will flow easier and make it more flexible.

Once the cake is iced, it is time to begin decorating. The way you hold the icing bag is important, as the direction and angle you hold the piping bag will influence the way the patterns and shapes you will create, will turn out. Thankfully there are only two positions to hold the piping bag to make certain designs.

The first position is to hold the piping bag at a 90 degree angle, straight up from the surface of the cake. This is used for the simpler decorations that don't involve a lot of movement in making the design such as the centre of rosebuds, adding eyes to a character or making stars and dots. The other position involves the piping bag being held at a 45 degree angle, or holding the bag half-way between straight up and the surface of the cake.

In this position you have more flexibility to create sweeping styles, and create shapes with your piping hand. You can use this angle for flower petals, or writing on the cake. Some of the piping tips, like the tips for basket weave, petal and ruffle, have ends that are irregular. There is a right and wrong way to hold the bag when working with them.

Now that you know the basics here are a few tips to start you on your way to making a decorated cake.

• **Basket Weave** - Using this technique will give the sides of your cake the look of a basket. You may want to practice on a piece of waxed paper until you feel confident enough to begin on the cake. Using the basket weave tip and an icing that is of medium consistency, take turns applying a vertical stripe, following it with a horizontal stripe across the vertical. Make sure the horizontal stripes are a bit longer so the vertical stripe will fit across it. Soon you will see a basket pattern become apparent.

• **Bows** - This technique will make your cake look like a wrapped gift. Use a flat tip and medium icing. Hold your bag at a 45 degree angle and sweep your bag left, making half of the bow. Make the same movement to the right, making a figure 8. Hold the bag and sweep downward and out from the centre of the bow, once on each side to make 2 streamers.

• **Lacework** - This technique is great for wedding or baby shower cakes. You should practice this technique to make sure you have good control before you use it in your cake decorating. Using thin white icing, hold the bag at nearly a 90 degree angle and very close to the surface of the cake. You will want to make a border so you will need to decide how far you want to go in from the edge and make an icing border.

Move the tip up down and around to make many similar shapes, do not touch or cross the other designs. Do this until the area is as full as you want it to be. Now you can go over the border on both sides with a thicker icing. You will be amazed at the lacework you have created.

What Icing to Use in Your Cake Decorating

Those of us who are into cake decorating, think of the beautiful icing designs when we think of cake. Icing is the finishing touch on cakes, cookies, and cupcakes. There are several different types of icing used in cake decorating. The choice of icing while cake decorating, will have a great deal to do with how the decorated cake will look.

Buttercream Icing: Buttercream is the icing that is used the most in cake decorating. This is the same type of frosting that we can buy readymade in the grocery store. This icing is easy to use and easy to make. The ingredients are confectioner's sugar, and butter or shortening. What you use to thin the frosting will differ with the icing texture you need to work with, to determine whether to use eggs or milk. Take care when thinning the frosting, remember, a little milk goes a long way. If you find the frosting is too thin, you can add a bit of confectioner's sugar to thicken it.

To ensure an even finish on your frosting, dip the icing spatula in cold water to make the surface smooth. This will give a smoother finish for writing. Buttercream is used to create flowers and other decorations made with a pastry bag. The icing needs to be the right consistency to make flower petals or writing. When you make roses out of icing, you can freeze them and add them to the cake later. This will make them easier to handle.

Buttercream can be stored in the refrigerator without getting hard. Make sure it is back to room temperature before you attempt to use it.

Foam Icing: This is a meringue and is used on lemon pie or Baked Alaska. This frosting is made of egg whites beaten into stiff peaks. It is possible to add flavouring and colour to the meringue. You will not be able to use this icing for intricate cake decorating, and you won't be able to use an icing bag with this icing. This icing is used when you want the cake to look fluffy, with little ornate decoration.

Glazes: This frosting is thin and watery, and will harden into a shell after it is placed on the cake. This frosting is mostly used on pastries. Glazes help to keep the pastry moist.

Fudge Icing: Fudge icing is made from chocolate, peanut butter, almond, or mint. This icing is quite thick and contains both shortening and butter.

Fondant: This icing is very popular with those who decorate wedding cakes, and cakes for very special occasions. The ingredients are simply powdered sugar, water, cream of tartar, or glucose. Fondant is thick and doughy, with a silky, smooth, texture. Fondant will give the cake a flawless surface, and soft, rounded edges. Working with fondant is an art and will take practice to get it right. Fondant has a translucent quality, and will work best when placed on the cake over a thin layer of buttercream frosting.

Flat Icing: This icing is similar to a glaze, but it is a bit thicker. Flat icing is a combination of confectioner's sugar and water and is used to drizzle onto pastries.

Royal Icing: This is also a flat icing, and hardens after it is set. Royal icing is a wonderful choice to make flowers, sculptures, and garnishes for cake decorating.

You can use any combination of the basic seven icings listed, to create a personal masterpiece. You will need to practice before you become good at cake decorating. You will get the hang of it sooner than you think, and even the mistakes will taste great.

Type of Fillings

Many people feel that cake filling can be difficult to maintain. If done right, you can make a beautiful filled cake, without too much drama.

Cake filling flavours need to compliment one another, chocolate with orange, hazelnuts, or almonds

Some cakes will not hold up well without refrigeration. Mousse and whipped cream can separate, get soggy and drip. Berries can get soggy and drip everywhere. Buttercream needs to be kept in a cool place so the frosting won't separate. Cakes covered with fondant should be kept at room temperature and never be refrigerated.

If you are using fresh berries or whipped cream as a filling, make sure the cake will be eaten within a few hours. If you are going to prepare a cake a couple of days in advance, you may want to use simple syrup or a flavour wash on the cake layers to keep the level of moisture up, before you add your filling.

Keep in mind the dietary restrictions of your guests. Make sure there is no conflict when you are decorating a cake for special occasions, or for a client. If diabetics are present, you might want to make or purchase a small dessert that is sugar free for these guests.

When you are making a cake for an occasion that is serving other food, make your flavours stronger and your colours brighter. This will make the cake stand out and your cake decorating will be something they will remember.

Cake Filling Ideas

- Buttercream icing flavours- Mocha, Orange, Raspberry, Chocolate, Lemon, and extra Almond extract.
- Any variety of jam.
- Mocha buttercream with a sprinkle of finely chopped heath bars, or with caramel sauce dribbled over the cake and sprinkled with chopped peanuts.
- Whipped cream, Chocolate Mousse, and Vanilla Custard.
- Almond, Lemon, Coffee, Raspberry, Hazelnut, or orange liqueur can be brushed on the   cake before icing, for a flavour boost.
- Flavoured Syrups are great for a flavour enhancer that is non-alcoholic. These syrups come in over 100 flavours.

To combat the problem of cake filling oozing out of the sides of the cake, try this. Use a jam that is all fruit (Polaner), Heat the entire jar in the microwave without the lid. After 30 seconds the jam should be warm and liquid. Stir a small package of Jelly that is the same flavour of the jam.

This will intensify the flavour of the jam, and best of all, once it is spread on the first layer and left alone for a few minutes, the jam will set. The second layer can be put on the cake without fear of spill-over. You may want to set the first layer into the freezer for about 15 minutes to make the jam set better.

This jam can be kept in the fridge and heated the next time you want to fill a cake. Don't keep it too long though.

You can also make a dam of buttercream around the edge of the cake to keep the filling where it is supposed to be. This way your icing will not become stained by the filling and your decorated cake will remain beautiful.

How to Make Your Icing Smooth and Even

When you make the cake, be sure that the batter is level in the pan before you place it in the oven. Check the cake at 20 minute intervals to make sure the cake is baking evenly, if you find one side of the cake is higher than the other, you should turn the pan around so it will rise evenly. If you find that your cake baked with one side higher, use a knife to even it. You should do this while the cake is warm.

The cake should be cooled for at least a day before you even think about starting any cake decorating. The outside of the cake could feel cool, but the middle of the cake may stay warm for hours. Frosting the cake before it is completely cool can ruin your decorating.

After the cake has cooled, turn it upside down on a cake board, you will have less crumbs this way. To avoid crumbs all together put a thin layer of icing on the cake. Once you have covered the cake with a thin layer of frosting, you can cover that layer with a normal layer of icing. Make sure the icing is smooth and even.

You can dip your metal icing spatula in cold water and go over the icing, this will smooth the icing beautifully.

Icing is the most important ingredient in cake decorating. The icing should be quite stiff, if it is too stiff to work with you can always thin it out. When you are making the frosting, make a good amount. You will need it for other decorations on the cake. Make sure you have plenty of food colouring, as you will need it to colour the icing for different cake decorations.

When you are ready to start decorating your cake you will need a few pieces of equipment. You will need more than one pastry bag, and the icing tips you will be using for the decorating you want to do. These items can be bought at craft stores and cake decorating supply store.

To start with, choose the tip you will be using first. Hold the pastry bag with the hole down and place the tip inside, as far as possible. You should use about a cup of icing in the bag at a time, and start it out in a bowl, that way you can thin the icing with a little milk if you need to, before you put it in the icing bag. The icing should be thin enough to go through the tip, but thick enough to make the designs you choose. If you are still a novice at cake decorating, you should practice making the decorations on waxed paper before you attempt to put them on the cake.

When you are ready to ice the cake, you will need to hold the bag with both hands and apply steady pressure. Applying a steady pressure assures that the icing the icing will come out in an even strip. Unless you are making a long strip of piping, you should place the bag closely over the cake start squeezing and count to three, then stop squeezing and lift the tip up and away from the cake. If this decoration looks the way you want it to, move on to the next one, if it isn't quite right, keep practicing.

If the cake decoration stays in the shape you intended, then you have the frosting at the right consistency. If it does not hold together, the icing is too thin, and if it was hard to push it through the tip or the cake decoration cracks, the frosting is too thick.

How to Apply Edible Cake Art

There are many edible cake art images available for cake decorating that will make your cakes stand alone in excellence. You must follow the directions carefully for best result and ease in application.

Tips to applying edible cake art:
- Make sure you have clean, dry hands before touching the image. If you are working with a frozen cake, let it thaw a bit before applying the icing. Edible Image(r) cake decorations need a bit of moisture to blend into the icing.

• If the cake is dry, spray it with a light mist of water, brush on light syrup, or add a thin layer of icing before you apply the image so it will stick to the cake. If your cake is moist, don't add water or moisture to the cake. Too much water will cause the colours to run.

• Once the image is applied, it cannot be removed or moved. Know exactly where you plan to place the image. Using care, apply the image to your cake, face up. Once the image has been applied, tap the image down gently with your fingertips. Start from the centre of the image and work toward the edges.

• If the image should become moist or hard to remove from the backing, it can be placed in the freezer for a couple of minutes, the image should peel off easily.

• If the image should bubble after it is applied, gently tap and DO NOT RUB the image. If the cake is still frozen after application, it should be placed in the refrigerator to thaw slowly. Avoid exposing the image to ultraviolet light. The image may fade over time, as with any food colouring.

• If the image bubbles during freezing, again you can gently tap the image.

Handling and Storage of the Image

- Edible Image decorations should be stored in the silver bag it came in, and kept in a cool, dry place.
- Make sure to reseal the original bag after you remove an image.
- You will need to use the image immediately after it is removed from the bag.
- Once you have finished decorating with Edible Image(r) decorations. You can store your product as you normally would. The images are freezer, shelf, and refrigerator friendly.

How to apply the Images to other products

- **Ice Cream:** To apply the image to a cake frosted with ice cream or non-dairy whipped topping, do not add any additional water. If you are applying the image directly on ice cream, you should let the ice cream melt just a bit before application. When you are working with soft serve ice cream, you will get better results if you apply the image while the ice cream is soft and then freeze it.
- **Buttercream icing:** Apply the image immediately after icing the cake. Buttercream will form a crust about an hour after they have been applied. If this has happened, spray the icing with a fine mist of water before you apply the image.

• **Frozen cakes:** Thaw a bit before icing to avoid cracks forming in the cake, then you can apply the image. If the decorated cake is frozen, you will need to let it thaw slowly in the refrigerator, uncovered, so the cake will not sweat and the colours will stay true.

• **Royal icing:** Make sure you add a good mist of water over a cake iced with royal icing before you apply the image

• **Non Dairy Whipped Topping:** When working with this medium, do not add any extra water before you apply the image. Keep the finished cake in the refrigerator to maintain the integrity of the image and the topping.

• **Poured White Chocolate, or other poured icings:** Apply the image while the icing is wet. Be sure your cake is on a flat surface or the image may slide.

• **Rolled Fondant or Sugar Paste:-** When placing an image over sugar paste or fondant, plan where you will put the image. With a small paintbrush, apply a good amount of plain water. Brush water only where the image will be. Any water outside the image will leave a mark on the fondant or sugar paste. Although you must be sure to apply enough water, or the image will not stick. Edges can be tapped down with a very small, slightly moist paintbrush.

Standard Instruction for Application

- Remove the Edible Image from the sheet just prior to application.

- If there are still images in the bag, reseal it immediately.

- Remove the image from the backing sheet by gently placing it on a table edge, (facing up) and rolling the backing sheet over the table edge. This will loosen the image so that it can be carefully peeled from the backing.

How to Make Candied Fruit for Cake Decorating

Making candied fruit is a simple process. You infuse fruits and citrus peelings in sugar syrup. You can candy orange wedges, orange peel, lemon peel, grapefruit peel, pineapple and fresh cherries. You can also candy fruits, such as carrots for carrot cake decorating.

You will need two sauce pans, one for making the syrup, and another to blanch the fruit. This is a recipe for candied orange peel.

Simple Syrup

This syrup is used for making candied fruits, adding flavour to cold drinks, and adding moisture to sponge cake. There are different strengths of simple syrup for different uses. Thin simple syrup, made with 1 part sugar to 2 parts water, is used to brush on cake layers, mostly sponge cake, to provide extra moisture and sweetness. Medium simple syrup is made with equal parts of sugar and water.

This is excellent for adding sweetness to mixed drinks, coffee, iced tea and to candy fruit. Syrup made of 2 parts sugar and 1 part water is used as a base for sorbet, and making rock candy.

Combine equal parts of sugar and water in a medium saucepan. Bring to a boil and let the sugar dissolve. You do not need to stir the syrup, but if you do it will do no harm. You can flavour the syrup.

Take the syrup off the heat and cool slightly. Stir in 1 or 2 tsp. of vanilla for a basic vanilla syrup. This syrup can be kept in a lidded jar in the refrigerator for up to a month.

Remove the bottom and top of an orange. Set the flat end of the orange on a cutting board. With a sharp paring knife, slice the peel off in strips, starting at the top and slicing downward, following the curve as much as possible. Don't worry about cutting off the white pith of the peel. Although it is usually bitter, blanching it will make it translucent and the syrup will sweeten it.

You can candy the peel as it is, or cut into strips that are 1/4 inch wide, to use in cake decorating and garnishes. You can also dip it in chocolate and use it for a snack. Larger peels, like grapefruit should be cut into strips for even cooking.

Place the peel in a pot of cool water. Bring water to a rolling boil, remove from heat and transfer the peel into a colander to drain. Repeat the process twice more. For grapefruit or a more tart flavoured fruit, you will need to blanch them seven or eight times. Cherry and pineapple do not need blanching and can be placed directly into the syrup. Between blanching taste the peel, if it is tender it has been blanched enough. Place the peel into the pot of syrup and bring to a low simmer. Let simmer for 15 to 30 minutes or until the orange rind becomes translucent and the peel tastes sweet and tender

Remove the pot from heat and let it cool. The orange rind can be stored in its own syrup for weeks in the refrigerator. You may choose to drain them and roll them in sugar. Sugared rinds tend to dry out quite fast and should be eaten within a couple of days. You can dry the peel and dip it in tempered chocolate to make it last a bit longer.

You can use the orange flavoured syrup in other drinks or dishes. Nothing really goes to waste!

Easy Solutions to Common Cake Decorating Mistakes

Anyone who has ever frosted a cake knows there are times when the icing will pull apart the top of the cake and cake crumbs get will into the frosting. To stop this from occurring, you should start with a crumb coat. This is the same icing that you are using to frost the cake, but it has been thinned down a bit. That way you will cover any part of the cake that might crumb with a thin layer of icing, and it will give you a base over which you will put a regular coat of icing. Take care that you do not make the icing too thin. It should be thinned down just enough to cover the cake without tearing it and picking up crumbs.

After you apply the crumb coat to the cake, you need to let it set about 2 hours or more before you apply the rest of the icing. In fact it should rest in the refrigerator, and can be kept there overnight before you need to add more icing. It is okay if you see crumbs in the crumb coat, they will be stuck in this first layer of icing and will not effect the next layer of icing. The cold will set the icing and it will be a cinch to ice after that.

There can be a problem with fillings spilling out the sides of the cake. There are ways to stop this from happening when your cake decorating involves a filled middle.

1. Bake your cake the day before you are planning to fill it. This will make the cake firmer and will give it time to settle. A freshly baked cake will be unstable and will not hold fillings as well as when they are settled.

2. You can also use icing to make a dam to stop the filling from spilling out. Once the dam has been made, you can frost the whole cake with a crumb coating. The cake should be set in the refrigerator for 2 to 3 hours, or overnight, this will firm up the icing and will keep the filling from oozing out the sides. The dams made of icing will firm up and keep the filling in.

If you don't have time to bake and decorate a cake all at once, you can bake the cake and freeze it until you need to decorate it. A cake can be kept in the freezer a couple of weeks before it needs to be used. You must prepare the cake for freezing by wrapping three layers of strong cling wrap around the cake, followed by one layer of aluminium foil just prior to freezing. If you do not follow this procedure, your cake will dry out and crumble. You will also need to make sure the cake is completely thawed before attempting to ice it.

You will need to allow the cake to defrost slowly, at room temperature, for one or two days until it has defrosted. Icing a cake before it has thawed will make the icing sweat and become mushy, this will ruin your cake decorating, and all your hard work will be for nothing.

Pricing Your Services

Pricing is so important to the success of your business. You are in a very competitive business and you will be judged on your prices compared with your competitors.

When pricing your cake look at the following costs:

- Buying your ingredients, including delivery costs or the cost of picking them up. Include the costs of your decorations, grease proof paper etc.
- Costs of your packing including your cake boxes, labels etc.
- You consumables such as cooking costs, washing your uniform, cloths, aprons etc.
- Designs, licences etc.
- A percentage of your cooking equipment costs.
- A percentage of your office equipment costs such as printers, computer, software etc.
- Add to this a reasonable profit that will keep you interested in decorating cakes for a living.

You should set some money aside to build up your brand image by advertising and training any staff or distributors. People are more likely to buy if they know the product and how great they are.

Will I Succeed?

You've got a great idea, you are pretty sure that what you have will sell; you've even got some cash together. Have you got what it will take to succeed? What else do you need?

Vision: You must be able to see where you are going and what the future will hold. See what others are not able to see and build your business on these visions.

Courage: The ability to act upon your vision despite having doubts. Having the courage to give up job security and a planned future for the opportunity of a successful new business.

Strategy: Having the courage to act upon your vision, you now need to build your strategies. You will need a business and a marketing strategy. These are the formulas that you will use to drive forward and manage your business.

Planning Skills: To ensure that you reach your vision, you need copious amounts of planning. Planning how you will reach your targets, how you will meet new changes and challenges and how you will improve your business. You will need a business plan and a marketing plan.

Researching: Having decided what your business is going to be, then you will need to find out who will want to buy from your business and at what price. This takes a fair amount of researching.

Conceptualising: Knowing what you want to sell and to whom, you now need to define your products and services. Brainstorm different things that you associate with your company. Include everything, good and bad, until you are out of ideas. Keep in mind that ideas generate ideas. Write everything down, this is how you move your company forward. Use this period to design your products, what you want your company to look like and how you want it to be perceived by your customers.

Creativity: You will need the ability to think outside of the box. Keep ahead of your competitors by coming up with new, unusual and unique concepts and solutions to their needs. You will need to create marketing materials, packaging and sales pitches – all will need verbal and visual creativity.

Determination: Along the way you will come across many hurdles and set backs, you will need to dig deep, make your changes and keep going. Determination and the belief in your visions and plans will keep you on the road to success.

Humour: When entire world seems against you and all seems to be going wrong, when your customers seem to be your worst enemy then you need a sense of humour to carry you forward.

Lastly you need good luck!

A Successful Business Start up

R ight you have sorted out your business ideas, you are ready to go ahead and you know what you want to sell and to whom. Now you need your business structure. These are all the things that make up your business. They include:

- **Legal Base:** This includes such factors as your licenses, insurances and setting up your company.

- **Your Market:** You need to decide who you want to market your services to and where they will be.

- **Your Services:** You now need to decide what services you are going to offer to these people, how you would like to package them and what prices you wish to charge.

- **Your Business Plan:** Whether you are looking for funding or not – a business plan is the foundation of a new business.

- **Your Funding:** You should now take your business plan and look around for funding, starting with your Bank.

- **Your Premises:** Look around for your new premises, preferably in the middle of your potential market. Remember that central to your success is the position you choose for your business. Foot traffic past your door and many potential customers within a short journey from your new business is vital to you finding customers.

• **Web Site:** Most businesses have them now – so even if you don't want to set one up now – at least buy and hold onto your domain name – in case someone else gets hold of it.

• **Your Staff:** Good staff that reflect your business ideals are vital so spend some time spend some time finding the best staff you can.

• **Marketing:** So important and so difficult to get right. Start with a good marketing strategy and go from there.

• **Grand Opening:** Make sure you make a splash and attract as much curiosity as possible.

Your Business Framework

W hen starting a business of what ever kind, large or small, there is a always a require framework or scaffolding that you have to set up. Not only does this make your business much more effective, but it also saves you from a lot of embarrassing and costly problems. When you start up your business, remember to tick off the 10 items below and you will have a very sound start to your business. Here is your framework:

- **Business Name.** Choose an appropriate name that sums up what your business stands for. It has to be unique – try and ensure that a suitable domain name is also available as you will probably want a web site as well. The owner of an established web site might cause problems if you give your brick based business the same name – so be careful in your choice.

- **Your Business Entity.** Obtain professional advice as whether to the best way to set up your business as a limited company, partnership etc. Then register your company.

- **Patents and** Trademarks. If you have unique products then you need to ensure that you have registered your patents before your start trading. Similarly any product names, mottos, selling tags etc should be trademarked. Take professional advice on how to do this.

- **Licenses and Permits.** Ensure that you have all the licenses and permits that you are legally required to have.

• **Insurance.** You may think that you don't need this but you do and will. So take out property, business, vehicle liability, staff and disaster insurance. A good broker can advise you.

• **Taxes.** A necessary evil I am afraid. Register with your local tax collector. Set up a good accounting system and hire a good accountant.

• **Employment Laws.** Establish what you local employment laws are and ensure that you adhere to them. Set up employee guidelines and handbooks. Make sure you hire and fire legally.

• **Banking.** Visit your local banks and find the best business bank account and credit card for you business. Always keep your business and personal spending separate.

• **Business Plan.** This is your carefully written plan on how you want your company to operate, what you want to sell, where and to whom. It includes your business and marketing strategy as well as your financial standing and projections. This is the foundation of your business.

• **Liquid Cash.** Ensure that you have enough money to carry your through the first few months of your business as well as any foreseeable troublesome times ahead.

The Nasties

Tax, Insurance and Licences these are the nasties of your business and all of them are compulsory! Look up your local state/county/country web site to see what licences you will need. Similarly your country's tax web site will tell you what taxes you will need to pay, how you register to pay them and what forms you will need to fill in to become legal. Don't attempt to work without them – there goes the way to a world of misery. Tax officials in particular, are trained to find and collect unpaid taxes and these are always combined with extra costs and penalties.

Operating your business in some countries will require you and your staff to be licensed before you can start work. This should be displayed on your premises or available for view by your customers.

You may also need a sales tax permit (USA and other sales tax based countries) or VAT registration (UK and some Europe and Asia) if you reach the VAT registration limit.

Do not forget that you will also need some kind of health licensing. Once again you need to check with your countries/local county/local state web site to see the health requirements and training you need. You will almost definitely need to keep a very clean and professional kitchen and utensils and will probably need some training in food handling and storeage.

Check List For Starting A New Business

You are ready to give up your job to start your new business, or even scarier, sink your savings into your new business. You just want to make sure that you have done everything possible to succeed, here is a check list for you.

1. Legal Stuff:
   - Do you have a memorable business name and the associated domain name?
   - Do you have a legal name and business entity?
   - Have you got all your licences?
   - Have you got all you certificates such as health and fire?
   - Have you registered everything you need to?
   - Have you told the tax department and got your numbers and details?
   - Are all your shares, statutory meetings etc correct?
   - Do you have all the patents and trademarks you need?
   - Do you have the legal documents on your premises – leases, sales, mortgages etc.?
   - Do you have all the posters and legal manuals etc that you need?

2. Strategies and Planning:
   - Do you have your Business Plan written?
   - Do you have a Business Strategy?
   - Do you have a Marketing Strategy?

• Have you decided upon what Business Model you will use?

3. Protection:

• Do you have your insurances for you, the company, liabilities, staff, premises and vehicles?

• Have you got health insurance for you and staff if necessary?

• Do you have your pension set up?

4. Finances:

• Are your finances in place and have you signed all the forms necessary?

• Do you have enough and on the right terms?

• Have you got your bank set up?

• Do you have your credit/debit card and payment processor set up?

5. Premises:

• Are your premises/office ready and equipped?

• Are all the utilities that you need connected – gas, electric, phone, broadband etc.?

• Do you have all the vehicles, computers and machinery that you need?

6. Staff:

• Do you have all the staff you need?

• Are they trained or ready to be trained?

• Do you have the necessary uniforms?

7. Marketing and Products:

- Have you checked who your potential market is and where these customers are hiding?

- Have you ensured that what you are selling is really, really what your proposed customers want?

- Do you have your pricing and upgrading sorted out?

- Do you have your branding sorted out?

- Do you have your starting marketing materials?

- Do you have standard replies to customer enquiries, invoices, receipts, business cards and letter heads sorted out?

How Much Does It Cost To Start A Business?

You've got your business idea, think that you will be able to get a good loan and even have your business plan being written but…. The one big burning issue is – How much does it cost to start a business?

Well you first of all have to be realistic and understand that you are unlikely to make a profit within the first six months of business – so you should also budget for your first six months running costs. So here is your shopping list:

1) **Purchase or rental of lease/franchise/premises.** This will include any Realtor fees, deposits and other legal expenses.   Even small businesses need some kind of premises. To start with you can use a home office, but you are going to need somewhere to hold all that stock and materials that you will soon need as you get bigger. If you intend to only rent somewhere then take into account any deposit you will need as well as at least six month's rental costs.

2) **Cost of fit out and purchase of new equipment.** This will include any work that needs to be done on your premises as well as any equipment you have to buy in order to start and run your business. Often you can lease equipment in order to mitigate high start up costs.   This also includes a car or van to deliver your stock to your distributors.

3) **Six months worth of advertising and marketing**. This will be particularly high at the start as you establish your business. Factor in some cold calling as well as a launch party or opening day. Marketing will include a lot of local advertising in order to attract good distributors.

4) **Legal, licensing and banking costs.** Your business will need to be set up correctly, licensed and have a good bank account. Sadly all of these require money. You may also need a payment processing service to use credit cards.

5) **Staff costs for six months.** Staff will be the basis of providing good service to your new customers. Make sure that you have enough money put aside to find them, train them and keep them! Much of your staff costs will be on a commission basis but you will still require admin staff and one or two "on staff" distributors and maybe warehouse staff as well. They will all want to be paid, often before you get paid for your sales.

6) **Uniforms, office and marketing supplies, packaging etc**. You will need to establish your brand. This means that your staff will need uniforms or at the least business cards and name tags. You will need brochures, adverts etc. If appropriate you will also need standardised packaging and documentation.

Your office will also need office equipment and supplies. You should also budget for designing your logo, brochures and adverts if you cannot do this yourself.

7) **Stock and supplies** – to keep you going for six months. This is a big expense because if you have 10 hosts they all need a core stock from which to sell from.

8) **Maintenance** for six months – your equipment will also need to keep going for six months. This includes your cars, computers, printers, copiers etc. Budget for a lot of printing ink!

9) **Any loans** that you have will also have to be paid. Again look at least at six months or until you break even and can pay the loan.

10) **Your salary** for six months – lastly you will need to pay your own bills and maintain your family during this time. You should expect that for a short while your standard of living will go down.

Add this up and add 10% for contingency and some good luck.

Profitable New Cake Decorating Business

Check List – Business Start Up Costs

Item	√
Purchase/Rental of lease/franchise/premises	
Realtor /Agent Fees	
Legal Fees	
Bank Fees	
Payment Processing Fees	
Business Consultancy Fees	
Business Planning Fees	
Deposits	
Business Equipment	
Office Equipment –fax, computer etc.	
Stock	
Office Stock – stationary, etc.	
Vehicle Detailing or sign writing	
Property Sign Writing	
Electric/Gas/Water/Phones	
Telecoms and internet	
Maintenance, Leasing and Hiring Fees	
Advertising and Marketing Costs	
Marketing Brochures, Business Cards etc.	
Design Costs	
Staff Costs	
Staff Uniforms	
Training	
Salary Costs	

Getting Started With Little Money

The age old question, you want to start your business but have little capital available. So how do you do it?

First of all have a look round for sources of borrowing money. The first obvious step is your bank. They are unlikely to lend money unless you have at least a deposit of 20%. Similarly if you approach the Small Business Bureau (USA) or Small Business Association (UK) or similar and ask for a guaranteed loan – they are probably going to want a similar deposit.

They may be able to offer you some advice as to where to go for funding. Your best bet is to get together a realistic business plan with what you wish to do and what it will cost in quite detailed format. Also include details of whom you expect your market to be and how large this market is.

A venture capitalist or angel investor is pretty much out of the question unless you have a really unique protected product or a very well established business.

Another source of business funding help may be to apply for a grant. They are difficult to get and you will have to have, not only a good case but a very well defined business idea.

Profitable New Cake Decorating Business

So if you are capital poor the best advice is to start small. Look at a smaller version of what you intend to start up. Start with offering your services to local businesses first and working from a home office. Start selling from a mall kart or stall in a flea market, boot sale or local market place. You can also try eBay, CraigsList etc.

Try offering your cakes as raffle prizes for charity. Attend as many wedding fairs as you can possible afford. Give out small sample cakes as well as your business plan. Go where brides congregate such as beauty salons and leave your business card. If you have a professionally printed business card with a picture of one of your cakes – even better. Make friends with wedding planners and florists. Offer to advertise them if they advertise you. Work with them or offer them commission for sales make through them. Think Bride and work out where they will be and make sure that you and your business cards are in the same place!

Start small and you have not risked too much. Build your business, establish your business name and build up capital and customers.

What Goes Into A Business Plan?

You are ready to write your business plan for funding purposes, or you are starting a new business and know that you need one. So what goes into your business plan?

Well first of all, a good, well structured business plan can be the foundation to your new company. It is important that you spend some time ensuring that it is accurate. Here are the relative portions of your business plan.

- **Executive Summary**. This will be the first thing read by your potential investor and a strong executive summary with an overview of all that is required will ensure that the rest of your business plan is read.
- **Business Overview** and structure including shares issued and who owns them. This is where you describe your physical business, your business model, your Mission Statement, objectives of the business and key milestones,
- **Business Strategies** including business, financial, marketing and exit strategy. This is an important part of your business plan and details how you are going to mange your future business. The business strategy is how you run your business and how you intend to expand and grow from a new business. The financial strategy is how you will manage your finances, when you will invest, how much will go into research, if you will lease or buy etc.

Your marketing strategy deals with marketing and advertising your business, to whom, how and at what costs. Your exit strategy is how the investor will be able to recoup their investment.

• **Markets**, which is who you expect to buy your products and services with some predictions of volumes.

• **Products**, which are the services and goods offered. You should include how they are manufactured or sourced as well as the fulfilment process.

• **Financials** such as costs, overheads, profit etc with realistic indications of why, how and when. You should also include your marketing and staffing budgets as well as overhead costs and your break even position.

• **Staffing** including resumes/CV's of major staff, brief terms of reference and an organisation chart.

• **The Way Forward**, what will happen in the future and how an investor will get their money back.

If you include all of these you will have a great business plan. This can seem daunting, which is why it can be worthwhile to employ a business planning consultant, who can also provide business consultancy. Good luck.

Meeting The Bank Manager

M eeting with your bank to ask for a loan for your business is always going to be a challenge even if you have a profitable business. Here are a few ideas for you.

It's important to remember that your loan manager is probably a kind human being who has to adhere to the bank's rules on lending. The basic ones are:

- That you can repay the loan.
- The loan is business based and for a reasonable reason.
- That your business is viable and bona fida business.

Go to the meeting armed with:

- Your business details such as licenses etc.
- An outline of your business and how you see it expanding in the next few years.
- If you are seeking a large amount of money or have a new business then you must have a business plan.
- How much money you require and when you need it.
- How you will spend it and on what items.
- How your business will benefit, expand or profit from the loan.
- What collateral you can offer the bank – don't offer this until asked.
- When and how you will repay the loan.

Try not to hide anything – evasion is not a good reflection on your business acumen. If you are asked a difficult question then answer it as honestly as you can – but by putting a good spin so that you sound positive.

Common Business Mistakes.

All entrepreneurs have to learn from their own mistakes as they build their business, but wouldn't it be great to have some one tell you what the common mistakes are and how to avoid them? You Want a Successful Business – So Don't Do This!

- **Believing that you will start earning straight away.** All businesses take time to establish themselves – even internet based ones. People need to know where you are, what you sell and most importantly, that they can trust your company to deliver what it promises. Expect to spend at least 6 months working away at your business before you break even – sometimes longer.

- **Believing that you can set up a business and it continually earns for you.** Even a very profitable business needs continual management to ensure that your profit does not erode. Your products and marketing need to continually change to meet the changing circumstances in the real world.

- **Believing in Get Rich Quick Schemes:** A good business is established by part inspiration, part perspiration and just a little bit of luck!

- **Believing that you can earn whilst you are aware from the office.** Even if you fully automate your business and hire really good staff, there is always an element of "while the cat is away". That is why there are so many "absent owner" sales.

• **Being a single product company.** As good as your product may be, markets and tastes will change and so must you. If your product is very good – other companies will quickly take action to seize your market share by bringing in similar products at cheaper prices.

• **Not offering upgrades and enhancements.** It is far easier and cheaper to sell to existing customers. You do this by offering upgrades and enhancements to their existing products. You should have a group of products at several increasing price points.

• **Relaxing after you success.** Businesses need continual effort, management and improvements. Although a product launch is hard work, you should start on your next product shortly afterwards. This will give you sustainable success and several income streams.

• **Believing that a business can be established with little capital.** Marketing, infrastructure purchases, stock, advertising and staff all cost money and must be purchased in order to make a profit. Cash flow kills more business than anything else.

- **Believing that you know all you have to**. Your competitors may have been in the business longer than you have, your customers may be very knowledgeable. Meeting customer needs is a constantly changing landscape and you need to keep up to date on the latest trends and technology. You need to be able to project yourself as an expert in the field you work in. If you do not have this knowledge then learn it or buy it in!

- **Not investing in your staff.** Your staff are the public face of your business. They should be well trained, knowledgeable and well dressed as well as fully motivated to sell on your behalf.

- **Not motivating** your staff. Good staff are hard to find and difficult to keep. They help your business expand and be profitable. They will grow your business exponentially as word of mouth spreads.

- **Branding.** It is important that your company is recognised and has a good image. This helps spread the word about your services! Otherwise why would your customers hire you? Spend on your brand, its worth it!

Learn these lessons well, avoid the mistakes at all costs you should save valuable time and resources by doing things right the first time.

Your Unique Selling Point

Y ou've heard about a Unique Selling Point and guess that you want one but you have no idea what it is and why you need one. Often called the U.S.P – it means – "What makes your company, product and services different from all the other companies selling the same thing?

Now obviously in a crowded business environment – be it click or brick – you want your company to not only stand out but be memorable. You USP will do this for you.

So how do I define my USP?

Have a look at you company and a few companies that you believe compete with you. Also look at a couple of companies who are trading as you would wish to trade in the next few years. For products we mean products, goods or services.

So, what product features could you have that would make you different from your competitors?

- Look at what products you sell the most often or most of.
- How do these products differ from each other?
- What benefits do these products provide?
- What better features do you/ you could provide?
- What features do competitor's products have that yours do not?

- What features do your products have that are different you're your competitors?

Make yourself stand out from your competitors and emphasise this in all your fully branded marketing materials and you should not only stand out from others but also look larger, more professional and memorable.

Branding, The How's, What's And Why's

Your business brand says a lot about you and your business. If you create a strong brand image, it will elevate you above your peers and provide a good model for your product and service development as well as a sound foundation from which to expand your business.

What is Branding?

Many people think that having a logo and maybe a short description of their services is all they need to set up their brand. This is not so.

Your brand encompasses all that your business does, from first contact with your potential customers through to how your products are defined and sold. Your brand is what defines and describes your business. Look at any two different companies that compete in the same market and look at how people recognise and remember them.

For example look at Rolls Royce and Toyota - they both sell cars but each company is known for a different reason. Someone looking for a car on a budget would not go to Rolls Royce - yet both sell their cars on reliability. Clearly more people would aspire to purchase a Rolls Royce, but many also be happy to purchase a Toyota.

Look again at the perceived value of a brand. Why is the iPod the desired MP3 product when other brands have similar properties and reliabilities? People perceive the ipod to be superior and are willing to pay more for the pleasure of owning one. Indeed many people would not consider any other purchase. This is clever branding by Apple who marketed their product as being very desirable to certain markets.

I Don't Have that Kind of Money

So why do I need to create my own brand? The main reason has to be to differentiate yourself. You are starting a business in a very crowded market so you need to stand out from the hobby workers and other competitors.

Branding also makes the promotion of your company and development of your products so much easier. There are thousands of new businesses and many times more web sites. You need to:

- Set yourself apart from the competition
- Make yourself memorable so that people will either look for your business or choose you above your competitors.
- When introducing your business to a new customer, your brand should go before you and communicate much of what you want to say.

Your cakes will be easier to define and design, if you centre them around your brand definition. For example if you are selling wedding cakes your brand image will be totally different than if you are selling party cakes. You need to appeal to a different market – i.e. young adults as opposed to young children and their parents.

So How Do I Create My Own Brand Then?

You brand must say:

- Who you are.
- What you do.
- How you do it.
- What the benefits of using your business are.

In order to be able to do this you must first be able to describe what you want your business and products say, so start with your Mission Statement or Elevator Statement.

- The Mission Statement - this is what you want your business to be or do as it operates. You need to be realistic and focused. Being profitable is not a mission statement, but deciding what you want to do to be profitable is.
- The Elevator Statement - This is 1-4 sentences that you would use to describe your business, in the time that it takes to travel in an elevator - or a few minutes. It is used when meeting new people who ask "and what do you do?" or as an introduction when networking.

What Should Be Described Within My Brand?

First of all, pretend that you are one of your target customers and list 5 things that they will be seeking from your product. These items would encompass a short definition of one of more of the following:

- Price.
- Quality.
- Service.
- Support.
- Scarcity or availability.
- How and when delivered.
- Accessibility.
- Security.

So now define who, what and where you are in these terms and you should come up with something like this as a Mission Statement.

"We will provide quality fantasy cakes to Suburbia. We will include fairies, dragons, elves, monsters and unicorns and have the widest selection we possible can."

Your elevator pitch might be something like this: "We provide quality character based cakes for children's parties via our shop and the internet."

Tag Line

Now need to be recognised by your customers. Here is where you tag line and logo come into play.

My tag line - what's that.
Well if you become as well known as Nike it can be something very short like "Just Do It" - but that is a few years and few £million down the road. Your tag line is a short description of what you do.

Something like "Cakes for weddings and parties" which explains what you sell and to whom. It also differentiates you from other companies in your area.

Logo's

Now you need a logo - it does not need repeating that this should also reflect your brand. If you are saying you are modern and efficient - you don't want an old fashioned, messy looking logo. It should always reflect your brand and be simple and recognisable. You should include it on:

- All your communications.
- Your web site.
- Your products.
- Your packaging.
- Your marketing and promotional materials.
- Your adverts.

Working with your brand

Your brand is so much more than your logo; it is your company name, your web site and the colours that you use.

Remember your brand allows you to pre-sell your company and products as well as ease the introduction of new products as you become more established. Be consistent with your brand promotion - don't keep changing it as people are more likely to remember things the more they see them. Regular marketing enables you to establish your credibility and relevance to your target market.

Branding, Packaging And Other Stuff

Everything that your customers and staff see should be "stamped" with your company brand and be instantly recognised as belonging to your company. Let us look at where your will be using your brand. Invoices and order forms should have your company details, contact details and web site as well as your logo.

Business Name

Pick a great business name that reflects the type of cakes you are selling and who you are selling to. If you are getting a domain name (and you should, even if you don't want a web site just yet) you need to match this with your company name.

Packaging

It stands to reason that all your bags and packaging, including that used in delivering your items, should be stamped with your company name, logo, phone number and web site. All packaging should include further Order Forms, and a catalogue.

Marketing Material

Once again you should market such that your company and how to contact it, is instantly recognisable. How and where you advertise should also back up your brand image. If you are selling family friendly items then you would not advertise in a "lad's mag" for example.

Starting Small With Your Premises

Sometimes circumstances dictate that you can't afford a retail shop but you really want to get your business started. Many small, retail businesses are not suitable to run from your home base or via a warehouse. Web sites, whilst having low start up costs, also take a lot of marketing and time to become profitable. Why not think about starting a kart or kiosk in a shopping mall? Here are a few points to consider.

Mall Karts and Kiosks

As always Location, Location, Location: The location of your business is crucial to its survival. A store's location can often spell its success or failure. Without sufficient store recognition, a business can suffer poor cash flow and will inevitably fail over time. Your business needs to be physically located out in midst of everyday life, in broad daylight where shoppers can easily find you.

The location itself of the mall plays a huge role in your kart's success. Is the mall located in an isolated part of the city or town, or right in the heart of the action?

You must forecast the level as well as the timing of traffic your business will receive during the morning, midday, and late afternoon on each day of the week. Therefore, you can efficiently establish an employment schedule as well as appropriate operating hours.

Choose your mall carefully so that it has ample traffic of potential customers. Go there with a "clicker" and see how many people pass by per hour. Visit on several different days of the week as well as at different times.

Quality of Traffic: It is one thing to have steady traffic, and another to have the kind of traffic that your business needs. Some malls attract low-to-middle income people; others are targeted towards the upper class. Choose wisely.

Position in the Mall: Your success in a mall will depend on whether you are located in a section that is conducive to what your business is selling. You should look at the *complementary nature of the adjacent stores.* The worst place you could be is by food store that sells celebration cakes. Look for businesses that are complimentary to what you are selling such party and wedding stores.

You may want to be located near a restaurant where people are already in their "hunger fulfilling" state of mind.

Similarly *high volume areas* where lines of patrons form, such as theatres or department stores, are also good mall locations as it could give potential customers several minutes to look in your display or listen to your sales pitch. People will hopefully spend while they wait – if not you have their undivided attention for some time and they will remember you.

Costs: Rental costs in shopping malls are often higher than rates in downtown Main Street. You main consideration should be: will the higher traffic compensate for the increased rental cost? If you can easily recover your monthly rental payment and overhead expenses, you're in a good position to make a profit.

People Buy with their Eyes! Ensure that you display your products in an tempting manner. Karts, kiosks, stalls and vans and are very good in selling items that are "impulse buys". Make your products appealing and your sales pitch interesting and your sales will increase!

Market Stalls and Boot Fairs

The same criteria about location appertains to market stalls and boot fairs. Obviously your outlay will be much smaller – but so will your potential income. Care should be taken to ensure that your stall looks professional and well branded otherwise your business will be classed as a "hobby business" and people will expect to pay correspondingly low prices.

Wedding Fairs

If you are chasing the bridal market, you must attend these fairs. Arrange your stall to attract the bride and groom. Bring your sample cakes as well as photos of others you can produce. Hand out pieces of cakes to be eaten and be prepared to make appointments for the bride and groom to talk to you about their cakes. They will not have long to talk to you at the fair so work on getting the appointemts.

Marketing From Your Retail Site

Whichever low cost option you chose, ensure that you have plenty of brochures available to give out to interested potential customers. Don't leave them on the counter otherwise you will go through a lot of them for little return – save them for the really interested people. You could leave business cards for anyone to take. You should display some good samples as well as a lot of items for sale. Be prepared to take orders or make appointments.

Marketing Your Business

The first thing you need to do is contact your friends and neighbours and see if they need your services or know someone who does.

Advertising: Set up an advert on your PC. You can print them off, on postcards quite easily. It should read something like this.

Beautiful and Unique Cakes

If you having a celebration why not have your own beautiful cake to help you celebrate? Prices you can afford.
Your satisfaction is always guaranteed!
Call CompanyX: 123-4567 - ABC Cakes

In essence, you have a professional advertising "billboard." Now is the time to use a bit of shoe leather. Put the cards on notice boards in supermarkets, shops, clubs, offices etc. Always ask first. You can also put a similar advert in your local papers if that is affordable.

Business Cards: If you also decided to use business cards – use the front to put your company name, contact details and a one line description of your services. Start to leave these wherever you are allowed to. Anywhere that busy people, future brides and new parents are found.

Selling Big: If you want to sell to clubs, societies, hotels etc then now is the time to "dial and smile". You need to get contact details from the yellow pages, internet or your contacts. Call them up or send them your Sales Pack, with the aim of obtaining an appointment to discuss your services. The next chapter explains what to do on this appointment.

Advertise on your Car: A great idea would be to have magnetic signs made for your company and services. Place these signs on the sides of the cars your people use for transportation to each job, and later on, to the sides of your company van or car.

Yellow Pages:- One other form of advertising you should go with would be a display ad in the yellow pages of your telephone directory.

Low Cost Retail: Look at getting yourself a stall at the local market, the car boot sale, a kiosk in the mall etc. which will get you a lot of exposure and hopefully some sales for little outlay. We go into this later in the book.

Find a Unique Way to Sell Your Cakes - Think about why people should come to you for their cakes instead of going to a bakery. Do your cakes taste better, are they more beautiful, do you offer a unique style, or do you provide better service (drop off cakes on the special day)? You may want to offer all of these things to get the customers coming to you.

Once they see the beautiful work you do, they will tell everyone they know and you will be able to get more business.

Use Press Releases: You should send a press release to local and nearby news papers every time you participate in non-profit or community events in your town. You should also send a press release if you have anything happen with your business. When you do, be sure to mention everything that makes your business unique. This will be a bit of advertisement along with the announcement.

Advertise in newspapers and shoppers: Make sure to advertise your business. You should take out a larger ad the month of May for graduation, in May and June for weddings, or when a big event is going to take place. Place ads in the high school paper, or if you have a college nearby, you can advertise in any paper they may have and on the bulletin board. Before you do think about what discounts or specials you can offer for these events. Make sure you specify that all orders need to be in by a certain date, this could prompt buyers to take action and order from you.

A Business Website: You should create a website for your cake decorating business. Make the site informative and easy to navigate. Show samples of your cake decorating skills, and mention how unique your business is, if you are flexible, and what type of cake decorating you do. You may or may not want to put prices on your website, sometimes it is better to have them call you and you can quote them a price, according to their needs. When you advertise, make sure you include your web address in your advertising.

Look for Distributors: One way to expand your business is to find other businesses who are willing to advertise your cake decorating business. Coffee shops and restaurants will probably be your best bet. This will give your business more exposure and save you from having to open a store of your own. In exchange for this service they would receive a commission on each order you receive from their establishment.

Barter with local party and event planners: You can strike up a bargain with local planners to show your portfolio to their customers. In exchange you can recommend them to your customers. Get included in their list of vendors, and they may have you making and decorating all of their cakes.

Offer Free Products for fund raisers, church activities, local events and festivals. Get involved in fundraising for local charities, school, church, and business events. By offering a free cake for these events, you will be gaining a great deal of advertising exposure. Make up brochures and hand them out when you are in attendance.

Real Estate Offering: Contact local Realtors and offer a special on housewarming cakes for their clients. Realtors often give a gift to clients when they sell a home. When you make cakes for these occasions, make sure to place the cake in a beautiful cake box imprinted with your business name, address, phone, and web address. You can also include a discount coupon if they order a cake within a certain time frame.

Referrals: Tell everyone you come into contact with about your business. Carry business cards with all of your information on it. Give them 2 or 3 cards and ask them to pass them along to others who might be interested in using your talents. You should also ask customers for referrals. Offer them a discount on their next cake if they can drum up new business for you.

It takes a short while to start up any kind of company. Start touting for small contracts to begin with particularly those that you can do yourself.

Interacting With Your Customers

Once you spread the word that you're in the business of decorating quality cakes you'll have no trouble at all keeping busy!

When prospective clients call or email you, explain your services and prices. When selling large or bespoke orders it is best to either ask for a 50% deposit or a 100% payment. This is because once you have finished the service; it is sometimes hard to obtain the payment due. Make sure that you receive all the payment due before you finish the service.

First Contact

When a prospective customer calls or your telephone sales pitch is positive, have your appointment book and a pen handy. Be friendly and enthusiastic. Explain what you do and offer to show a few samples.

When they ask how much you charge, simply give them a wide range and say that you will give a firm cost quote, once you've discussed their requirements. Then without much of a pause, ask if 4:30 this afternoon would be convenient for them, or if 5:30 would be better.

You must pointedly ask if they can come to make your cost proposal at a certain time, or the decision may be put off, and you may come up with a "no sale." You may prefer to invite them to visit you if you have a suitable reception area.

Just as soon as you have an agreement on the time and place to make you cost proposal and marked it in your appointment book, ask for their name, address and telephone number.

Jot this information down on a 3 by 5 card, along with the date and the notation: Prospective Customer. Then you file this card in a permanent card file.

Save these cards, because there are literally hundreds of ways to turn this prospect file into real cash, once you've accumulated a sizeable number of names, addresses and phone numbers. If you have a suitable computer program, then enter the details there as well.

Estimating

When you go to see your prospect in person, always be on time. A couple of minutes early won't hurt you, but a few minutes late will definitely be detrimental to your closing the sale. If they are coming to you then ensure that you give good directions and are ready for them.

Always be well groomed. Dress as a successful business owner. Be confident and sure of yourself; be knowledgeable about what you can do as well as understanding of the prospect's needs and wants. Do not smoke, even if invited by the prospect. It's important to appear methodical, thorough and professional

A little small talk after the sale is appropriate, but becoming too friendly is not. You create an impression, and preserve it, by maintaining a business-like relation ship.

When you go to make your cost estimate, take along a ruled tablet on a clipboard a calculator, your appointment book and your sample designs.

You should also have at least two of your sales packs (one for the customer and the other for their friend that may also need your services) and a blank contract (more of this later). A receipt book would also be a good idea. You can buy folios in stationary stores that will keep these all tidy.

If they choose one of your sample designs, fine, but if they want a particular design of their own, now is the time to ask for photos or start jotting down all their requirements, including sizes and colours.

You should hopefully come up with a drawing of what they require in front of them. Get them to sign off these details and picture so that there is no dispute later. You will probably have to come back to them with a firm price. Make sure that it is possible for you to actually produce the cake!

Discuss when they need the cake/s and if you are delivering it/them or if they are collecting from you.

Now complete the contract for them, summarising what you have just agreed and confirm that you will send her a typed up list of all the cake details you have just completed. Ask them for confirmation on the contract and for a deposit. Also offer them a sales pack for their friend who may need your services.

The Art of Selling

It has been said that a sale is really closed long before the seller makes the final pitch to the customer. In many ways, this is very true. Many customers make a decision to buy in five minutes or less of being introduced to the product. As a successful entrepreneur, it is up to you to make those five minutes really count.

There are a couple of important things that take place in this five minute window of opportunity.

First, the customer decides whether or not it is worth the time to learn more about the product. If the answer is no, then even thirty minutes of a great pitch will accomplish nothing.

Second, the customer will think of major obstacles that will prevent the purchase from taking place. If a customer decides the product is out of reach for some reason, that will make everything that follows that first five minutes of no value whatsoever.

Your job is to overcome both these issues and encourage the prospect to not only desire the product, but also be able to visualise actively using the product to great advantage.

Here are a few ideas on how to accomplish this:

- **Ascertain the needs of your client.** This means asking clarifying questions that help to narrow the focus of the presentation to what is important to the customer. For example, if a primary need of the client is to pay the phone bill at the end of the month, tailor the presentation to show how the product can directly help achieve that goal.

- **Be prepared to address common obstacles.** Many obstacles are not unique – people from all sorts of background will share the same concerns. Proactively bring those up during those first five minutes and quickly demonstrate how they are non-issues. This will make it possible to dispose of those concerns and hold the attention and interest of the prospect past that five minute window.

- **Always close with benefits**. Some of those benefits may have to do with overcoming obstacles, but go a little further than that. Using the phone bill example again, point out how the product can make it easier every month to pay the bill – not just the one that is due the end of this month.

Making the most of those first five minutes will greatly increase your chances of closing the sale. Spend some time working on a model presentation and critique the results. This will help you move with greater prowess when the real deal comes along. Congratulations you have just made a sale!

Buying And Selling Wholesale

Clubs, churches, restaurants, hotels, school, teams and many other groups buy custom cakes for their organisations either for their own celebrations or to raffle or sell on. They usually do this through wholesale because it is considerably cheaper that way. This is a great market for you to get into and you should spend some of your marketing time in chasing this work. Of course your prices will be lower for a large order, but you will save time in setting up the designs.

In order to meet these needs, or as you get bigger you will need to buy your ingredients wholesale. To most people, the word wholesale equates to being inexpensive. The larger quantity of items you need, the lower the price goes. Before buying anything wholesale you want to check out the prices of everyone that offers that option.

Check around your neighbourhood for wholesalers and join them. Check their prices against those that you can get in local supermarkets and on line – they are not always cheaper. What they can offer though, is cheaper prices when you buy large quantities. Before you buy a couple of hundred pounds of flour, be sure that you have the appropriate space to store your cooking items in a cool, child and animal free environment.

Administration

Administration is very important. Without good administration your company will quickly disintegrate into chaos and you won't know who has what and who needs to pay for services and who needs them to be cleaned and when. Your administration should include ways of controlling or managing the following:

- Collecting money from your customers

- Banking money.

- Managing enquiries and complaints.

- Invoice and bill payment.

- Accounts and book keeping including, payroll, banking, taxes and VAT/taxes.

- Purchasing and auditing equipment. At least once a year and preferably quarterly, equipment must be checked against your accounts and for the need to be repaired.

- Salary and commission payments.

- Staff training and development.

It may seem a lot, but if you start small and get yourself a good accounts package, a good accountant and bank manager it is a lot easier.

Customer Administration

- Set up a file for each of your customers with their contact details, what you have agreed to do, the price to be charged and any other details. Keep a folder/file for each customer. Add each order to the file – latest order on top. The file should include all contact details. If you have a number of orders per client put a list of orders on top and tick them off as you complete them. If you have a lot of customers have a customer number format.

- You should also keep a record of money due and paid. You should be able to find a good accounting system very easily. Always give a receipt and chase overdue accounts.

- Make a To-Do list of all your orders and tick off those that have been completed. Put in order of importance/when delivered.

- Keep a detailed diary of when they have to be delivered by. In the diary also note what extra services were requested and what payment you need for the service.

Writing A Winning Proposal?

You've been working with a potential client and you think that you finally have the future project all worked out – then they ask you for a proposal. You've seen this great potential project but you need to bid for it. So how do you write that proposal that is going to win you the business?

Well first of all let's look at what the proposal should do. Win of course, but before that you have to:

- Make your company stand out from the others as well as reflect the values and brand of your company.
- Offer the solution that is required in a format that is easily understood.
- Be well priced so as to attract the client, provide a profit for your company as well as opportunities for you both to work together in the future.
- Be well structured, well written and well presented.

Bearing in mind the above, your proposal should look something like this:

1) Thanks for the opportunity.

2) Your understanding of the job that needs to be done.

3) How you would complete the job, how long it will take and who will do it.

4) Why your company is the best for the job.

5) Your price – with subject breakdowns if appropriate.

6) Any "must haves" assumptions made etc in getting to the price.

7) Last thanks and way forward.

Item 5 and 6 should be on their own page so that they can be removed if necessary.

Remember to put your company details and contact details on the header of each page and your copyrights, date and page number of number of pages on each footer.

When you send off the proposal, on time of course, include a brief cover letter, with:

- Your contact details.
- The name of the person who is their contact for this bid.
- Your thanks for the opportunity.
- A very brief overview of bid - no price.
- A time frame that bid is current.
- Your thanks and hope to hear from them soon.

Now sit back and pride yourself on a job well done. Good luck

Putting Your Business On The Internet

Just about anyone can put a web site up on the internet and now days it is quite easy. You have two choices as how to set up your website:

- As a shop window for your company, with contact details etc.
- As a fully working site with ecommerce facilities.

Which ever option you choose, you first need a god domain name. Go to a good domain provider like enom, godaddy, namecheap and spend under £10 on a domain. Choose a domain name that has the word "cake" and preferably "cake decoration" in it. This will help with your search engine positioning as well as act as a memory jog to your potential customers.

As A Shop Window

Hop over to hostgator or similar and then buy a monthly hosting account. With that will come a site maker - where you can easily set up a web site using one of thousands of templates. You can add payment processor linkages, forums etc.

As A Full Site

You will probably need to get this especially written and designed for you. Put your project on sites like guru/elance/scriptlance etc and find a competitive quote.

Get yourself a PayPal account or similar so that you can take payment on your web site. This is much more secure and quicker than taking checks.

Factors To Remember

Always consider your target market when designing your web site. Include some helpful information about your subject matter but nothing that will give away what you are trying to sell! Ensure that your contact details can be freely found and that details of your company and services are clearly set out.

As you will be asking for money before you deliver something – make your potential customer feel comfortable making payment and tell them what will happen next.

Respond to all enquiries and purchases very quickly. If this is difficult then set up an autoresponder to confirm you have received their enquiry/payment and will get back to them within a few hours. Place references that you have received from past

An Internet Marketing Strategy

Ok, you've got your web site set up, you are sure that it is search engine friendly and you are pretty certain what your customers want. You've identified at least 3 products that you want to promote and you think that they meet your potential customer's needs. So now what?

Well unfortunately the days, that I can remember, of "build it and they will come" have long gone. Unless you promote your web site – no one will know that you are there and no visitors means no sales. So where so you go from here?

Well take a deep breath, a pen and paper and let's start on your Marketing Strategy. Briefly for a new business, with a relatively inexperienced marketer, your strategy will probably include the following options:

- Pay Per Click Advertising
- Article Marketing
- Email Marketing
- Community Marketing
- Classified Advertising

Let's get started – and before you start panicking, you are just writing your Marketing Strategy. This course will explain how to do all of the following.

Your Advertising Kit

For each of your programs/products

1. Write a short advert – say 50 words.
2. Write a very short advert – say 15 words
3. Write a short article – say about 400 – 600 words.
4. Decide on your keywords – say about 30 – 50 words.

Your Marketing Kit

For your web site theme

1. Write at least 6 short auto responder messages.
2. Find or write at least 2 giveaway products.

Your Marketing Tools

1. Your web site
2. An autoresponder
3. A good email account

Put all of these together into your first Marketing Strategy.

1. **Submit your web site to all the major search engines.** This will start to get your web site noticed. As this takes a long time, it needs to be the first thing that you do. You can do this yourself or pay someone else to do this for you. We provide this service for our customers for £20 a month, which includes submission to Google, Yahoo and MSN.

2. **Set up your autoresponder form** on your web site and load your messages into the autoresponder. Ensure that you offer one of the giveaway products as a bonus for signing onto your ezine. The second giveaway can be set up for message 3 or 4. Your messages should be sent in the following intervals. Day 1,3,7,7,7,7

3. **Set up your download pages**, for your bonus products as well as the products you are selling. Ensure that you provide an extra offer on each download page.

4. **Submit your article** – including your resource box, to about 6 major ezine article sites. Limit yourself to 6 at the moment. Each of these submissions, if accepted will give you a link to your web site. If too many links to your new web site appear very quickly, search engines assume that you have been using "black hat" SEO tactics (a total no no) and will not list your site.

5. **Identify 4 forums** that discuss the topics of your web site. Set yourself up an account name that describes you well. We use the name "Biz Guru" which is our trade mark and name. Set up your signature to include your web site address. You now have 4 good links to your web site.

6. **Answer Questions:** Start answering questions asked within the forums. Do NOT post adverts for your web site or products. Use this time to establish your credentials. If you answer questions well and contribute to the forums, your web site tag will be noticed.

7. **Set up a PPC campaign** – you can start with the smaller search engines first. Take your very small advert and your keywords and use them in your campaign. Most search engines will help you with your choice of keywords. Remember to set a budget and test, test and test again until you get quality and converting traffic.

8. **Set up some classified ads.** You can do this one of two ways: i) choose one or two major sites/email lists and advertise with them. ii) use an ezine ad blaster to send your ad out to numerous low quality places.

9. **Test, Update and Modify.** Review, change and add to your PPC keywords. Submit more articles and adverts. Start tactfully promoting your products in the forums.

Your challenge will be to be listed in the major search engines and then get traffic. Now market your web site like mad. It will take several months to make an impact in the major search engines. So build up your local custom whilst you are doing this. www.GetIntoGoogleFast.com – Does exactly what is says in the domain!

Staff

Expansion means growth, involving people working for you, more jobs to sell, and greater profits. Don't let it frighten you, for you have gained experience by starting gradually. After all - your aim in starting a business of your own was to make money, wasn't it? And expanding means more helpers so you don't have to work your self so hard!

So, just as soon as you possibly can, recruit and hire other people to do the work for you. The first people you hire should be people to handle customer sales.

You can obtain good staff by word of mouth, advertising in your local Job Centre, supermarket etc. Look in your local university and local school and ask amongst friends. You will find a lot of people who want to work part time here - as well as those that are able to work early in the morning or in the evening if you need them.

You can start these people at minimum wage or a bit above, and train them to complete every job assignment in a set timeframe. You might consider hiring people on a contract basis so that if they don't work you don't pay. You don't get loyalty here though.

You should also outfit them in a kind of uniform with your company name on the back of their T shirts.

Customer Contracts

When you're dealing with customers, sometimes things can go wrong. It might be your fault, it might be their fault or it might be no-one's fault -- but if you didn't make a contract, then you'll all suffer.

Why Do I Need Contracts?

A contract gives you a sound legal base for your business, and some guarantee that you're going to get paid for your work without you having to ask the customer for payment in advance. In the event of a dispute, the contract lays down what the agreement was so that you can point to it and say what was agreed. If you ever end up having to go to court (let's hope you won't), the contract is what the judge's decision will be based on.

Without a contract, you leave yourself vulnerable and open to exploitation. Someone could claim that the terms they agreed with you were different to what you say they were or that they never signed up for anything at all and so they won't pay.

It's especially common to see big businesses mistreat small ones, thinking that they won't have the knowledge or the money to do anything about it. Essentially, contracts take away your customers' ability to hold non-payment over your head, and give you the ability to hold it over theirs instead.

Written and Verbal Contracts

It is important to point out the distinction in the law between a verbal (spoken) contract and a proper, written one. A verbal contract is binding in theory, but in practice can be very hard to prove. A written contract, on the other hand, is rock-solid proof of what you're saying.

You might think that you're never going to get into a dispute with your customers, but it's all too common to find yourself in a little disagreement.

They will often want to get you to do some 'small' amount of extra work to finish the job or make it better; not realising that doing so would completely obliterate your profit margin.

For this reason, you should be very wary of doing anything with nothing but a verbal contract. On the other hand, if you were incautious or too trusting and only got a verbal contract, it could still go some way towards helping you, especially if there were witnesses.

Won't It Be Expensive?

Written contracts don't necessarily need to be formal contracts, which are drawn up by a lawyer with 'contract' written at the top and signed by both parties.

These kinds of contracts are the most effective, but can be expensive to have produced, not to mention intimidating to customers.

The most common kind of written contract, oddly enough, is a simple letter. If you send a customer a letter laying out your agreement before you start work, and they write back to agree to it, that is enough to qualify as a written contract, with most of the protections it affords. It is best to get confirmation from your customer that they have received this contract.

If you are doing high-value work for some clients, though, it could be worth the time and trouble of having your lawyer write a formal contract, or at least of doing it yourself and getting a lawyer to look it over.

Formal contracts will give you more protection if the worst happens, and there's nothing to stop you from making it a one-off expense only by re-using the same contract for multiple customers. **PLEASE: TAKE PROFESSIOANAL ADVICE.**

Contracts for Small Purchases.

Obviously it would be silly to expect everyone who buys some £10 product or service from you to sign a contract, or write back indicating their agreement to your terms. In this situation, you should have a statement of the 'terms and conditions' that your customer is agreeing to by buying from you, and they should have to tick some kind of box indicating their agreement before you send anything.

The Top 5 First-Year Mistakes

Even once you've got past the starting-up stage, there are still plenty mistakes to be made, and most of them are going to be made in your make-or-break year -- the first one. Here are the top five things to avoid.

Waiting for Customers to Come to You

Too many people wait for their customers to phone, or come to the door, or whatever. They get one or two customers through luck, but nothing like enough to even begin paying their costs. These people sit around, looking at their competitors doing lots of business, and wonder what they're doing wrong.

You can't be like this. You have to go out there and actively try to find customers. Talk to people, call them, meet with them -- whatever you do, don't just sit there!

Spending Too Much on Advertising

So everyone tells you that the only way to get ahead in business is to advertise. Well, that's true, but you need to make sure that you stick to inexpensive advertising methods when you're starting out. Spending hundreds of dollars for an ad in the local newspaper might turn out to get you very few new customers, and you will have spent your entire advertising budget on it.

Make your money go further with leaflets, direct mail or email -- these are easily targetable campaign methods with high response rates and low costs. Remember that it is always better to spend money on an offer than on an ad, and always better to spend money on an ad than on a delivery method.

Being Too Nice

When you're running your own business, it can be tempting to be everyone's friend, giving discounts at the drop of a hat and making sure that you don't hassle or inconvenience anyone.

That's all well and good, until you find that your Good Samaritan act has just halved your profit margin without lowering the cost to the customer by very much at all.

Sometimes, you need to realise that you've got to be harsh to make a profit. Give people discounts to encourage them to buy or to come back, not because you like them or feel sorry for them. Don't be afraid to be ruthless in your pursuit of business success. Nice guys don't finish last, but they are running in a different race -- one with much less prize money. If that doesn't bother you, of course, then feel free to go for it.

Not Using the Phone

You'd be surprised just how common phone fears are -- if you're scared of the phone, you're not alone by any means. Many people are terrified of making phone calls, and avoid them wherever possible. I have seen more than one business owner reduced to tears on the phone and trying desperately to hide it from the customer.

You need to try your best to overcome your fears, as talking to customers on the phone is almost as good as meeting them for real. Letters and emails are useless by comparison. The best way to overcome phone fears varies from person to person, but it can often be as simple as making the phone fun, by calling friends and relatives often for a while and getting used to it. Alternatively, try working in telemarketing for a while -- if that doesn't make normal phone use look like a walk in the park by comparison, then nothing will.

Hiring Professionals for Everything

It can be tempting to think that, since you're starting out, you should just find a company or person to do every little thing you need. People seem to especially overspend on design services.

You might think it'd be great to have fancy graphics all over your website, but would it really increase sales? If I saw it, it would put me right off. Likewise, a slick brochure often fails to say anything more than 'I'm going to charge you a premium to pay for my expensive brochures'.

Don't hire someone unless you can demonstrate that the service they're going to provide will increase your profits by more than the amount you're spending -- if you're not sure, try it yourself first, and you can always upgrade it later.

Problems You May Have

As in any business you will get problems, sometimes just knowing what you may face is a great help.

• Some customers use office email to correspond with you. Make sure that you are discrete with the headings used on the emails to them.

• Some customers are never satisfied. Just make any reasonable changes that are requested. Similarly some have a very high opinion of their very basic experience. Be polite and patient.

• Some customers may have problems explaining what they want – this is where your product sheet comes in handy. Make sure that you write down everything that they request and get this agreed to.

• Some customers are very slow in replying – ensure that you give them a time limit to reply and then send two further reminders – telling them when the last one is.

Time for a Holiday: But How?

When you've been working long and hard at your business for a while, you might feel like you've earned yourself a little break. There are business owners out there who haven't taken a real holiday since they started their business -- including some who started their business as long as five years ago!

After all, how can you ever just desert your business and your customers and go bronze yourself on the beach? How can you avoid being on call 24/7 throughout your holiday? Well, everyone deserves some time to themselves at least once a year, if they want to keep being productive and avoid stress. Here's what to do.

Tell People When You Are Going Away.

You can't just disappear when you're running a business -- you need to let people know long in advance that you're not going to be available, and make sure that they have everything they need to manage without you while you're away. It's best to schedule your holiday not to interfere too much with the business.

However much you might want to have your holiday in the summer, it's important to remember that every business has its quiet months, and you should schedule your holiday in the period where they seem to be.

Change Your Voicemail Message.

A quick and simple way to let people know that you've gone away is to change your voicemail message. This allows you to still hear what people have to say when you get back, and stops them from wondering why you never seem to answer your phone.

A good format for the message is as follows: 'Hi, this is [your name] at [company name]. I'm sorry I'm not in the office right now, but I will be back on [give a date]. If you leave a message, I will be sure to get back to you'.

If you work from home don't give a coming back date unless you want to invite the local thief into your home!

Set Up an Email Auto responder.

Similar to a voicemail message, but less commonly used, is the email auto responder. Again, you don't want people to wonder why their emails are going unanswered, so your best bet is to set up your email program to automatically reply to any email you get with a message saying that you've gone away.

Example: 'Hello, and thank you for your email. This is an auto responder, as I'm away on holiday until [date]. I have received your email, however, and will respond to it upon my return. I apologies for any inconvenience to you, and I am willing to make an offer of 10% off your next order to make it up to you.' The special offer for people who get the auto responder is a nice touch -- it makes them feel lucky that they emailed you while you were away, instead of frustrated.

Don't Stay Away Too Long.

Of course, when you go on holiday, you're relying on people being willing to wait for you. That means you can't really take the kids to Disney World for two weeks, or spend a month staying with a friend abroad -- it's just too long to be away from your business for.

You should regard a weekend away as ideal (it avoids the whole problem for the most part), and a week as the maximum you can allow yourself. Don't let people make you feel bad about only taking one-week holidays: after all, you could always have more than one each year.

Alternatively: Get Someone to Look after the Business.

If you really want to get away for longer, or it's essential that your customers don't have any break in service, then you could consider getting someone to look after your business.

This could be an existing member of staff that you make your 'deputy', to be in charge while you're away, or it could be someone who's related to you and has some experience running a business. You could even hand the business over to a competitor that you're friendly with and share the profits with them, if you think they're trustworthy and they could handle it.

Enjoy your holiday!

In Conclusion

One of the most important aspects of this business is asking for, and allowing your customers to refer other prospects to you. All of this happens, of course, as a result of your giving fast, dependable service. You might even set up a promotional notice on the back of your business card (to be left as each job is completed) offering five dollars off their next bill when they refer you to a new prospect.

This is definitely a high profit business, requiring only an investment of time and organisation on your part to get started. With a low investment, little or no over head requirement, and no experience needed, this is an ideal business opportunity with a growth curve that accelerates at an unprecedented rate. Think about it. If it appeals to you, set up your own plan of operations and go for it! The profit potential for an owner of this type of business is outstanding! Good Luck.

Brought to You by the Biz Guru
"If you need help with your business – click or brick – we're here to help"

www.StartMyNewBusiness.com

Index:

Lightning Source UK Ltd.
Milton Keynes UK
UKOW021926281211

184462UK00012B/106/P